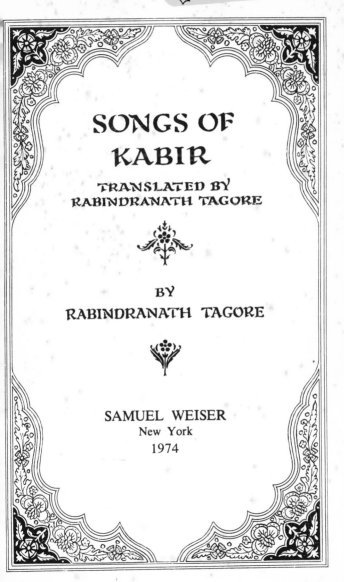

SONGS OF
KABIR

TRANSLATED BY
RABINDRANATH TAGORE

BY

RABINDRANATH TAGORE

SAMUEL WEISER
New York
1974

First published 1915
This paperback edition 1974
by Samuel Weiser, Inc.

ISBN 0-87728-271-4
Library of Congress Catalog Card No. 74-82318

Printed in U.S.A. by
NOBLE OFFSET PRINTERS, INC.
New York, N.Y. 10003

INTRODUCTION

THE poet Kabīr, a selection from whose songs is here for the first time offered to English readers, is one of the most interesting personalities in the history of Indian mysticism. Born in or near Benares, of Mohammedan parents, and probably about the year 1440, he became in early life a disciple of the celebrated Hindu ascetic Rāmānanda. Rāmānanda had brought to Northern India the religious revival which Rāmānuja, the great twelfth-century reformer of Brāhmanism, had initiated in the South. This revival was in part a reaction against the increasing formalism of the orthodox cult, in part an assertion of the demands of the heart as against

the intense intellectualism of the Ve-
dānta philosophy, the exaggerated
monism which that philosophy proclaimed.   It took in Rāmānuja's
preaching the form of an ardent personal devotion to the God Vishnu, as
representing the personal aspect of the
Divine Nature: that mystical "religion of love" which everywhere makes
its appearance at a certain level of
spiritual culture, and which creeds and
philosophies are powerless to kill.

Though such a devotion is indige-
nous in Hinduism, and finds expression
in many passages of the Bhagavad
Gītā, there was in its mediæval revival a large element of syncretism.
Rāmānanda, through whom its spirit is
said to have reached Kabīr, appears to
have been a man of wide religious culture, and full of missionary enthusiasm.
Living at the moment in which the
impassioned poetry and deep philoso-

phy of the great Persian mystics, Attār, Sādī, Jalālu'ddīn Rūmī, and Hāfiz, were exercising a powerful influence on the religious thought of India, he dreamed of reconciling this intense and personal Mohammedan mysticism with the traditional theology of Brāhmanism. Some have regarded both these great religious leaders as influenced also by Christian thought and life: but as this is a point upon which competent authorities hold widely divergent views, its discussion is not attempted here. We may safely assert, however, that in their teachings, two — perhaps three — apparently antagonistic streams of intense spiritual culture met, as Jewish and Hellenistic thought met in the early Christian Church: and it is one of the outstanding characteristics of Kabīr's genius that he was able in his poems to fuse them into one.

A great religious reformer, the founder of a sect to which nearly a million northern Hindus still belong, it is yet supremely as a mystical poet that Kabīr lives for us. His fate has been that of many revealers of Reality. A hater of religious exclusivism, and seeking above all things to initiate men into the liberty of the children of God, his followers have honoured his memory by re-erecting in a new place the barriers which he laboured to cast down. But his wonderful songs survive, the spontaneous expressions of his vision and his love; and it is by these, not by the didactic teachings associated with his name, that he makes his immortal appeal to the heart. In these poems a wide range of mystical emotion is brought into play: from the loftiest abstractions, the most other-worldly passion for the Infinite, to the most intimate and personal realiza-

tion of God, expressed in homely
metaphors and religious symbols
drawn indifferently from Hindu and
Mohammedan belief. It is impossible
to say of their author that he was
Brāhman or Sūfī, Vedāntist or Vaishnavite. He is, as he says himself,
" at once the child of Allah and of
Rām." That Supreme Spirit, Whom
he knew and adored, and to Whose joyous friendship he sought to induct the
souls of other men, transcended whilst
He included all metaphysical cate-
gories, all credal definitions; yet each
contributed something to the descrip-
tion of that Infinite and Simple Total-
ity Who revealed Himself, according
to their measure, to the faithful lovers
of all creeds.

Kabīr's story is surrounded by con-
tradictory legends, on none of which
reliance can be placed. Some of these
emanate from a Hindu, some from a

Mohammedan source, and claim him by turns as a Sūfī and a Brāhman saint. His name, however, is practically a conclusive proof of Moslem ancestry: and the most probable tale is that which represents him as the actual or adopted child of a Mohammedan weaver of Benares, the city in which the chief events of his life took place.

In fifteenth-century Benares the syncretistic tendencies of Bhakti religion had reached full development. Sūfīs and Brāhmans appear to have met in disputation: the most spiritual members of both creeds frequenting the teachings of Rāmānanda, whose reputation was then at its height. The boy Kabīr, in whom the religious passion was innate, saw in Rāmānanda his destined teacher; but knew how slight were the chances that a Hindu guru would accept a Mohammedan as disciple. He therefore hid upon the

steps of the river Ganges, where Rāmānanda was accustomed to bathe; with
the result that the master, coming
down to the water, trod upon his body
unexpectedly, and exclaimed in his
astonishment, "Rām! Rām!" — the
name of the incarnation under which he
worshipped God. Kabīr then declared
that he had received the mantra of
initiation from Rāmānanda's lips, and
was by it admitted to discipleship. In
spite of the protests of orthodox Brāhmans and Mohammedans, both equally
annoyed by this contempt of theological landmarks, he persisted in his
claim; thus exhibiting in action that
very principle of religious synthesis
which Rāmānanda had sought to establish in thought. Rāmānanda appears to have accepted him, and
though Mohammedan legends speak
of the famous Sūfī Pīr, Takkī of Jhansī,
as Kabīr's master in later life, the

Hindu saint is the only human teacher
to whom in his songs he acknowledges
indebtedness.

The little that we know of Kabīr's
life contradicts many current ideas
concerning the Oriental mystic. Of
the stages of discipline through which
he passed, the manner in which his
spiritual genius developed, we are completely ignorant. He seems to have
remained for years the disciple of
Rāmānanda, joining in the theological
and philosophical arguments which his
master held with all the great Mullahs
and Brāhmans of his day; and to
this source we may perhaps trace his
acquaintance with the terms of Hindu
and Sūfī philosophy. He may or may
not have submitted to the traditional
education of the Hindu or the Sūfī
contemplative: it is clear, at any rate,
that he never adopted the life of the
professional ascetic, or retired from the

world in order to devote himself to
bodily mortifications and the exclusive pursuit of the contemplative life.
Side by side with his interior life of
adoration, its artistic expression in
music and words — for he was a skilled
musician as well as a poet — he lived
the sane and diligent life of the Oriental craftsman. All the legends agree
on this point : that Kabīr was a weaver,
a simple and unlettered man, who
earned his living at the loom. Like
Paul the tentmaker, Boehme the cobbler, Bunyan the tinker, Tersteegen
the ribbon-maker, he knew how to
combine vision and industry; the
work of his hands helped rather than
hindered the impassioned meditation
of his heart. Hating mere bodily austerities, he was no ascetic, but a married man, the father of a family — a
circumstance which Hindu legends of
the monastic type vainly attempt to

conceal or explain — and it was from out of the heart of the common life that he sang his rapturous lyrics of divine love. Here his works corroborate the traditional story of his life. Again and again he extols the life of home, the value and reality of diurnal existence, with its opportunities for love and renunciation; pouring contempt upon the professional sanctity of the Yogi, who "has a great beard and matted locks, and looks like a goat," and on all who think it necessary to flee a world pervaded by love, joy, and beauty — the proper theatre of man's quest — in order to find that One Reality Who has "spread His form of love throughout *all* the world." [1]

It does not need much experience of ascetic literature to recognize the boldness and originality of this attitude in such a time and place. From the

[1] Cf. Poems Nos. XXI, XL, XLIII, LXVI, LXXVI.

point of view of orthodox sanctity, whether Hindu or Mohammedan, Kabīr was plainly a heretic; and his frank dislike of all institutional religion, all external observance — which was as thorough and as intense as that of the Quakers themselves — completed, so far as ecclesiastical opinion was concerned, his reputation as a dangerous man. The "simple union" with Divine Reality which he perpetually extolled, as alike the duty and the joy of every soul, was independent both of ritual and of bodily austerities; the God whom he proclaimed was "neither in Kaaba nor in Kailāsh." Those who sought Him needed not to go far; for He awaited discovery everywhere, more accessible to "the washerwoman and the carpenter" than to the self-righteous holy man.[1] Therefore the whole apparatus of piety, Hindu and Moslem

[1] Poems I, II, XLI.

alike — the temple and mosque, idol
and holy water, scriptures and priests
— were denounced by this inconven-
iently clear-sighted poet as mere sub-
stitutes for reality; dead things inter-
vening between the soul and its love —

The images are all lifeless, they cannot speak:
        I know, for I have cried aloud to them.
The Purāna and the Korān are mere words:
        lifting up the curtain, I have seen.[1]

This sort of thing cannot be tolerated
by any organized church; and it is
not surprising that Kabīr, having his
head-quarters in Benares, the very
centre of priestly influence, was sub-
jected to considerable persecution. The
well-known legend of the beautiful
courtesan sent by the Brāhmans to
tempt his virtue, and converted, like
the Magdalen, by her sudden encounter
with the initiate of a higher love, pre-
serves the memory of the fear and dis-

[1] Poems XLII, LXV, LXVII.

like with which he was regarded by the
ecclesiastical powers. Once at least,
after the performance of a supposed
miracle of healing, he was brought
before the Emperor Sikandar Lodī,
and charged with claiming the possession of divine powers. But Sikandar
Lodī, a ruler of considerable culture,
was tolerant of the eccentricities of
saintly persons belonging to his own
faith. Kabīr, being of Mohammedan
birth, was outside the authority of the
Brāhmans, and technically classed with
the Sūfīs, to whom great theological
latitude was allowed. Therefore,
though he was banished in the in-
terests of peace from Benares, his life
was spared. This seems to have
happened in 1495, when he was nearly
sixty years of age; it is the last event
in his career of which we have definite
knowledge. Thenceforth he appears
to have moved about amongst various

cities of northern India, the centre of a group of disciples; continuing in exile that life of apostle and poet of love to which, as he declares in one of his songs, he was destined "from the beginning of time." In 1518, an old man, broken in health, and with hands so feeble that he could no longer make the music which he loved, he died at Maghar near Gorakhpur.

A beautiful legend tells us that after his death his Mohammedan and Hindu disciples disputed the possession of his body; which the Mohammedans wished to bury, the Hindus to burn. As they argued together, Kabīr appeared before them, and told them to lift the shroud and look at that which lay beneath. They did so, and found in the place of the corpse a heap of flowers; half of which were buried by the Mohammedans at Maghar, and half carried by the Hindus to the holy

city of Benares to be burned — fitting
conclusion to a life which had made
fragrant the most beautiful doctrines
of two great creeds.

II

The poetry of mysticism might be
defined on the one hand as a tempera-
mental reaction to the vision of Reality :
on the other, as a form of prophecy.
As it is the special vocation of the mystical consciousness to mediate between
two orders, going out in loving adoration towards God and coming home to
tell the secrets of Eternity to other
men ; so the artistic self-expression of
this consciousness has also a double
character. It is love-poetry, but love-
poetry which is often written with a
missionary intention.

Kabīr's songs are of this kind : out-
births at once of rapture and of charity.
Written in the popular Hindī, not in

the literary tongue, they were deliberately addressed — like the vernacular poetry of Jacopone da Todì and Richard Rolle — to the people rather than to the professionally religious class; and all must be struck by the constant employment in them of imagery drawn from the common life, the universal experience.   It is by the simplest metaphors, by constant appeals to needs, passions, relations which all men understand — the bridegroom and bride, the guru and disciple, the pilgrim, the farmer, the migrant bird — that he drives home his intense conviction of the reality of the soul's intercourse with the Transcendent.   There are in his universe no fences between the "natural" and "supernatural" worlds; everything is a part of the creative Play of God, and therefore — even in its humblest details — capable of revealing the Player's mind.

This willing acceptance of the here-and-now as a means of representing supernal realities is a trait common to the greatest mystics. For them, when they have achieved at last the true theopathetic state, all aspects of the universe possess equal authority as sacramental declarations of the Presence of God; and their fearless employment of homely and physical symbols — often startling and even revolting to the unaccustomed taste — is in direct proportion to the exaltation of their spiritual life. The works of the great Sūfīs, and amongst the Christians of Jacopone da Todì, Ruysbroeck, Boehme, abound in illustrations of this law. Therefore we must not be surprised to find in Kabīr's songs — his desperate attempts to communicate his ecstasy and persuade other men to share it — a constant juxtaposition of concrete and meta-

physical language; swift alternations
between the most intensely anthropomorphic, the most subtly philosophical,
ways of apprehending man's communion with the Divine.   The need for this
alternation, and its entire naturalness
for the mind which employs it, is rooted
in his concept, or vision, of the Nature
of God; and unless we make some attempt to grasp this, we shall not go far
in our understanding of his poems.

Kabīr belongs to that small group of
supreme mystics — amongst whom St.
Augustine, Ruysbroeck, and the Sūfī
poet Jalālu'ddīn Rūmī are perhaps the
chief — who have achieved that which
we might call the synthetic vision of
God.   These have resolved the perpetual opposition between the personal
and impersonal, the transcendent and
immanent, static and dynamic aspects
of the Divine Nature; between the
Absolute of philosophy and the "sure

true Friend" of devotional religion.
They have done this, not by taking
these apparently incompatible concepts
one after the other; but by ascending
to a height of spiritual intuition at
which they are, as Ruysbroeck said,
"melted and merged in the Unity,"
and perceived as the completing opposites of a perfect Whole. This pro-
ceeding entails for them — and both
Kabīr and Ruysbroeck expressly ac-
knowledge it — a universe of three
orders: Becoming, Being, and that
which is "More than Being," *i.e.*, God.[1]
God is here felt to be not the final
abstraction, but the one actuality.
He inspires, supports, indeed inhabits,
both the durational, conditioned, finite
world of Becoming and the unconditioned, non-successional, infinite
world of Being; yet utterly transcends
them both. He is the omnipresent

[1] Nos. VII and XLIX.

Reality, the "All-pervading" within
Whom "the worlds are being told like
beads." In His personal aspect He
is the "beloved Fakīr," teaching and
companioning each soul. Considered
as Immanent Spirit, He is "the Mind
within the mind." But all these are at
best partial aspects of His nature,
mutually corrective : as the Persons in
the Christian doctrine of the Trinity
— to which this theological diagram
bears a striking resemblance — represent different and compensating experi-
ences of the Divine Unity within which
they are resumed. As Ruysbroeck
discerned a plane of reality upon which
"we can speak no more of Father, Son,
and Holy Spirit, but only of One Being,
the very substance of the Divine Persons"; so Kabīr says that "beyond
both the limited *and* the limitless is
He, the Pure Being." [1]

[1] No. VII.

Brahma, then, is the Ineffable Fact compared with which "the distinction of the Conditioned from the Unconditioned is but a word": at once the utterly transcendent One of Absolutist philosophy, and the personal Lover of the individual soul — "common to all and special to each," as one Christian mystic has it. The need felt by Kabīr for both these ways of describing Reality is a proof of the richness and balance of his spiritual experience; which neither cosmic nor anthropomorphic symbols, taken alone, could express. More absolute than the Absolute, more personal than the human mind, Brahma therefore exceeds whilst He includes all the concepts of philosophy, all the passionate intuitions of the heart. He is the Great Affirmation, the font of energy, the source of life and love, the unique satisfaction of desire. His creative word is the *Om* or "Everlasting Yea." The negative philosophy which strips from the Divine Nature all Its attributes and — defining Him only by that which He is not — reduces Him to an "Emptiness," is abhorrent to this most vital of poets. Brahma, he says, "may never be found in abstractions." He is the One Love who pervades the world, discerned in His fullness only by the eyes of love; and those who know Him thus share, though they may never tell, the joyous and ineffable secret of the universe.[1]

Now Kabīr, achieving this synthesis between the personal and cosmic aspects of the Divine Nature, eludes the three great dangers which threaten mystical religion.

First, he escapes the excessive emotionalism, the tendency to an exclusively anthropomorphic devotion,

[1] Nos. VII, XXVI, LXXVI, XC.

which results from an unrestricted cult of Divine Personality, especially under an incarnational form; seen in India in the exaggerations of Krishna worship, in Europe in the sentimental extravagances of certain Christian saints.

Next, he is protected from the soul-destroying conclusions of pure monism, inevitable if its logical implications are pressed home: that is, the identity of substance between God and the soul, with its corollary of the total absorption of that soul in the Being of God as the goal of the spiritual life. For the thorough-going monist the soul, in so far as it is real, is substantially identical with God; and the true object of existence is the making patent of this latent identity, the realization which finds expression in the Vedāntist formula "That art thou." But Kabīr says that Brahma and the creature are

"ever distinct, yet ever united"; that
the wise man knows the spiritual as
well as the material world to "be no
more than His footstool."[1] The soul's
union with Him is a love union, a mut-
ual inhabitation; that essentially dual-
istic relation which all mystical religion
expresses, not a self-mergence which
leaves no place for personality. This
eternal distinction, the mysterious
union-in-separateness of God and the
soul, is a necessary doctrine of all
sane mysticism; for no scheme which
fails to find a place for it can represent
more than a fragment of that soul's
intercourse with the spiritual world.
Its affirmation was one of the distin-
guishing features of the Vaishnavite
reformation preached by Rāmānuja;
the principle of which had descended
through Rāmānanda to Kabīr.

Last, the warmly human and direct

[1] Nos. VII and IX.

apprehension of God as the supreme
Object of love, the soul's comrade,
teacher, and bridegroom, which is so
passionately and frequently expressed
in Kabīr's poems, balances and controls
those abstract tendencies which are in-
herent in the metaphysical side of his
vision of Reality : and prevents it from
degenerating into that sterile worship
of intellectual formulæ which became
the curse of the Vedāntist school. For
the mere intellectualist, as for the mere
pietist, he has little approbation.[1] Love
is throughout his "absolute sole Lord" :
the unique source of the more abundant
life which he enjoys, and the common
factor which unites the finite and infinite worlds. All is soaked in love :
that love which he described in almost Johannine language as the
"Form of God." The whole of creation is the Play of the Eternal Lover ;

[1] Cf. especially Nos. LIX, LXVII, LXXV, XC, XCI.

the living, changing, growing expression of Brahma's love and joy. As these twin passions preside over the generation of human life, so "beyond the mists of pleasure and pain" Kabīr finds them governing the creative acts of God. His manifestation is love; His activity is joy. Creation springs from one glad act of affirmation: the Everlasting Yea, perpetually uttered within the depths of the Divine Nature.[1] In accordance with this concept of the universe as a Love-Game which eternally goes forward, a progressive manifestation of Brahma — one of the many notions which he adopted from the common stock of Hindu religious ideas, and illuminated by his poetic genius — movement, rhythm, perpetual change, forms an integral part of Kabīr's vision of Reality. Though the Eternal and Absolute is

[1] Nos. XVII, XXVI, LXXVI, LXXXII.

ever present to his consciousness, yet
his concept of the Divine Nature is
essentially dynamic. It is by the symbols of motion that he most often tries
to convey it to us : as in his constant
reference to dancing, or the strangely
modern picture of that Eternal Swing
of the Universe which is "held by the
cords of love." [1]

It is a marked characteristic of mystical literature that the great contempla-
tives, in their effort to convey to us the
nature of their communion with the
supersensuous, are inevitably driven to
employ some form of sensuous imagery :
coarse and inaccurate as they know
such imagery to be, even at the best.
Our normal human consciousness is so
completely committed to dependence
on the senses, that the fruits of intuition itself are instinctively referred to
them. In that intuition it seems

[1] No. XVI.

to the mystics that all the dim crav-
ings and partial apprehensions of
sense find perfect fulfilment.   Hence
their constant declaration that they *see*
the uncreated light, they *hear* the celestial melody, they *taste* the sweetness
of the Lord, they know an ineffable
fragrance, they feel the very contact of
love. "Him verily seeing and fully
feeling, Him spiritually hearing and
Him delectably smelling and sweetly
swallowing," as Julian of Norwich has
it. In those amongst them who de-
velop psycho-sensorial automatisms,
these parallels between sense and spirit
may present themselves to consciousness in the form of hallucinations: as
the light seen by Suso, the music heard
by Rolle, the celestial perfumes which
filled St. Catherine of Siena's cell, the
physical wounds felt by St. Francis
and St. Teresa. These are excessive
dramatizations of the symbolism under

which the mystic tends instinctively
to represent his spiritual intuition to
the surface consciousness. Here, in
the special sense-perception which he
feels to be most expressive of Reality,
his peculiar idiosyncrasies come out.

Now Kabīr, as we might expect in
one whose reactions to the spiritual
order were so wide and various, uses
by turn all the symbols of sense. He
tells us that he has "seen without
sight" the effulgence of Brahma, tasted
the divine nectar, felt the ecstatic contact of Reality, smelt the fragrance of
the heavenly flowers. But he was
essentially a poet and musician:
rhythm and harmony were to him the
garments of beauty and truth. Hence
in his lyrics he shows himself to be,
like Richard Rolle, above all things a
musical mystic. Creation, he says
again and again, is full of music: it *is*
music. At the heart of the Universe

"white music is blossoming": love
weaves the melody, whilst renunciation
beats the time. It can be heard in the
home as well as in the heavens; discerned by the ears of common men as
well as by the trained senses of the
ascetic. Moreover, the body of every
man is a lyre on which Brahma, "the
source of all music," plays. Everywhere Kabīr discerns the "Unstruck
Music of the Infinite" — that celestial
melody which the angel played to St.
Francis, that ghostly symphony which
filled the soul of Rolle with ecstatic joy.[1]
The one figure which he adopts from
the Hindu Pantheon and constantly
uses, is that of Krishna the Divine
Flute Player.[2] He sees the supernal
music, too, in its visual embodiment, as
rhythmical movement: that mysterious dance of the universe before the

[1] Nos. XVII, XVIII, XXXIX, XLI, LIV, LXXVI,
LXXXIII, LXXXIX, XCVII.   [2] Nos. L, LIII, LXVIII.

face of Brahma, which is at once an act of worship and an expression of the infinite rapture of the Immanent God.[1]

Yet in this wide and rapturous vision of the universe Kabīr never loses touch with diurnal existence, never forgets the common life. His feet are firmly planted upon earth; his lofty and passionate apprehensions are perpetually controlled by the activity of a sane and vigorous intellect, by the alert common-sense so often found in persons of real mystical genius. The constant insistence on simplicity and directness, the hatred of all abstractions and philosophizings,[2] the ruthless criticism of external religion: these are amongst his most marked characteristics. God is the Root whence all manifestations, "material" and "spiritual," alike proceed; and God is the only need of

---

[1] Nos. XXVI, XXXII, LXXVI.
[2] Nos. LXXV, LXXVIII, LXXX, XC.

man — "happiness shall be yours when
you come to the Root." [1] Hence to
those who keep their eye on the "one
thing needful," denominations, creeds,
ceremonies, the conclusions of philosophy, the disciplines of asceticism, are
matters of comparative indifference.
They represent merely the different
angles from which the soul may ap-
proach that simple union with Brahma
which is its goal; and are useful only
in so far as they contribute to this
consummation. So thorough-going is
Kabīr's eclecticism, that he seems by
turns Vedāntist and Vaishnavite, Pan-
theist and Transcendentalist, Brāhman
and Sūfī. In the effort to tell the
truth about that ineffable apprehension,
so vast and yet so near, which controls
his life, he seizes and twines together
— as he might have woven together
contrasting threads upon his loom —

[1] No. LXXX.

symbols and ideas drawn from the most violent and conflicting philosophies and faiths. All are needed, if he is ever to suggest the character of that One whom the Upanishad called "the Sun-coloured Being who is beyond this Darkness": as all the colours of the spectrum are needed if we would demonstrate the simple richness of white light. In thus adapting traditional materials to his own use he follows a method common amongst the mystics; who seldom exhibit any special love for originality of form. They will pour their wine into almost any vessel that comes to hand: generally using by preference — and lifting to new levels of beauty and significance — the religious or philosophic formulæ current in their own day. Thus we find that some of Kabīr's finest poems have as their subjects the commonplaces of Hindu philosophy and religion: the

Līlā or Sport of God, the Ocean of
Bliss, the Bird of the Soul, Māyā, the
Hundred-petalled   Lotus,   and   the
"Formless Form."   Many, again, are
soaked in Sūfī imagery and feeling.
Others use as their material the ordi-
nary surroundings and incidents of
Indian life : the temple bells, the ceremony of the lamps, marriage, suttee,
pilgrimage,   the   characters   of   the
seasons;   all felt by him in their
mystical aspect, as sacraments of the
soul's relation with Brahma.   In many
of these a particularly beautiful and
intimate feeling for Nature is shown.[1]

In the collection of songs here trans-
lated there will be found examples which
illustrate nearly every aspect of Kabīr's
thought, and all the fluctuations of
the mystic's emotion : the ecstasy, the
despair, the still beatitude, the eager
self-devotion, the flashes of wide illumi-

[1] Nos. XV, XXIII, LXVII, LXXXVII, XCVIII.

nation, the moments of intimate love.
His wide and deep vision of the universe, the "Eternal Sport" of creation
(LXXXII), the worlds being "told like
beads" within the Being of God (XIV,
XVI, XVII, LXXVI), is here seen bal-
anced by his lovely and delicate sense of
intimate communion with the Divine
Friend, Lover, Teacher of the soul
(X, XI, XXIII, XXXV, LI, LXXXV,
LXXXVI, LXXXVIII, XCII, XCIII;
above all, the beautiful poem XXXIV).
As these apparently paradoxical views
of Reality are resolved in Brāhma,
so all other opposites are reconciled
in Him : bondage and liberty, love and
renunciation, pleasure and pain (XVII,
XXV, XL, LXXXIX). Union with
Him is the one thing that matters to
the soul, its destiny and its need (LI,
LII, LIV, LXX, LXXIV, XCIII,
XCVI) ; and this union, this discovery
of God, is the simplest and most natural

of all things, if we would but grasp it
(XLI, XLVI, LVI, LXXII, LXXVI,
LXXVIII, XCVII). The union, however, is brought about by love, not by
knowledge or ceremonial observances
(XXXVIII, LIV, LV, LIX, XCI);
and the apprehension which that union
confers is ineffable — "neither This
nor That," as Ruysbroeck has it (IX,
XLVI, LXXVI). Real worship and
communion is in Spirit and in Truth
(XL, XLI, LVI, LXIII, LXV, LXX),
therefore idolatry is an insult to the
Divine Lover (XLII, LXIX) and the
devices of professional sanctity are
useless apart from charity and purity
of soul (LIV, LXV, LXVI). Since all
things, and especially the heart of
man, are God-inhabited, God-possessed
(XXVI, LVI, LXXVI, LXXXIX,
XCVII), He may best be found in the
here-and-now: in the normal, human,
bodily existence, the "mud" of material

life (III, IV, VI, XXI, XXXIX, XL, XLIII, XLVIII, LXXII). "We can reach the goal without crossing the road" (LXXVI) — not the cloister but the home is the proper theatre of man's efforts: and if he cannot find God there, he need not hope for success by going farther afield. "In the home is reality." There love and detachment, bondage and freedom, joy and pain play by turns upon the soul; and it is from their conflict that the Unstruck Music of the Infinite proceeds. "Kabīr says: None but Brahma can evoke its melodies."

III

This version of Kabīr's songs is chiefly the work of Mr. Rabīndranāth Tagore, the trend of whose mystical genius makes him — as all who read these poems will see — a peculiarly sympathetic interpreter of Kabīr's

vision and thought. It has been based
upon the printed Hindī text with
Bengali translation of Mr. Kshiti Mohan Sen ; who has gathered from many
sources — sometimes from books and
manuscripts, sometimes from the lips
of wandering ascetics and minstrels —
a large collection of poems and hymns
to which Kabīr's name is attached, and
carefully sifted the authentic songs
from the many spurious works now
attributed to him. These painstaking
labours alone have made the present
undertaking possible.

We have also had before us a manu-
script English translation of 116 songs
made by Mr. Ajit Kumār Chakravarty
from Mr. Kshiti Mohan Sen's text,
and a prose essay upon Kabīr from
the same hand. From these we have
derived great assistance. A considerable number of readings from the
translation have been adopted by us ;

whilst several of the facts mentioned
in the essay have been incorporated
into this introduction. Our most grate-
ful thanks are due to Mr. Ajit Kumār
Chakravarty for the extremely gener-
ous and unselfish manner in which he
has placed his work at our disposal.

E. U.

The reference of the headlines of the
poems is to:

Śāntiniketana; Kabīr by Śrī Kshiti-
mohan Sen, 4 parts, Brahmacharyā-
śrama, Bolpur, 1910–1911.

For some assistance in normalizing
the transliteration we are indebted to
Professor J. F. Blumhardt.

Sir Rabindranath Tagore
From a Drawing by W. Rothenstein

KABIR'S POEMS

I

I. 13.   *mo ko kahān dhūnro bande*

O SERVANT, where dost thou seek Me?

Lo! I am beside thee.

I am neither in temple nor in mosque:
   I am neither in Kaaba nor in Kailash:

Neither am I in rites and ceremonies, nor in Yoga and renunciation.

If thou art a true seeker, thou shalt at once see Me: thou shalt meet Me in a moment of time.

Kabir says, "O Sadhu! God is the breath of all breath."

II

I. 16.   *Santan jāt na pūcho nirguṇiyān*

IT is needless to ask of a saint the caste to which he belongs;

For the priest, the warrior, the trades-
man, and all the thirty-six castes,
alike are seeking for God.
It is but folly to ask what the caste of
a saint may be;
The barber has sought God, the washerwoman, and the carpenter —
Even Raidas was a seeker after God.
The Rishi Swapacha was a tanner by
caste.
Hindus and Moslems alike have
achieved that End, where remains
no mark of distinction.

III

I. 57. *sādho bhāī, jīvat hī karo āśā*

O FRIEND! hope for Him whilst
you live, know whilst you live,
understand whilst you live: for
in life deliverance abides.
If your bonds be not broken whilst
living, what hope of deliverance
in death?

It is but an empty dream, that the soul
   shall have union with Him because
   it has passed from the body:
If He is found now, He is found then,
If not, we do but go to dwell in the City
   of Death.
If you have union now, you shall have
   it hereafter.
Bathe in the truth, know the true Guru,
   have faith in the true Name!
Kabir says: "It is the Spirit of the
   quest which helps; I am the slave
   of this Spirit of the quest."

IV

I. 58.   *bāgo nā jā re nā jā*

DO not go to the garden of flowers!
   O Friend! go not there;
In your body is the garden of flowers.
Take your seat on the thousand petals
   of the lotus, and there gaze on the
   Infinite Beauty.

V

I. 63. *avadhū, māyā tajī na jāy*

TELL me, Brother, how can I renounce Maya?

When I gave up the tying of ribbons,
still I tied my garment about me:

When I gave up tying my garment,
still I covered my body in its folds.

So, when I give up passion, I see that
anger remains;

And when I renounce anger, greed is
with me still;

And when greed is vanquished, pride
and vainglory remain;

When the mind is detached and casts
Maya away, still it clings to the
letter.

Kabir says, "Listen to me, dear Sadhu!
the true path is rarely found."

VI

I. 83.   *candā jhalkai yahi ghaṭ māhīn*

THE moon shines in my body, but
   my blind eyes cannot see it:
The moon is within me, and so is the
   sun.
The unstruck drum of Eternity is
   sounded within me; but my deaf
   ears cannot hear it.

So long as man clamours for the *I* and
   the *Mine*, his works are as naught:
When all love of the *I* and the *Mine* is
   dead, then the work of the Lord
   is done.
For work has no other aim than the
   getting of knowledge:
When that comes, then work is put
   away.

The flower blooms for the fruit: when
   the fruit comes, the flower withers.

The musk is in the deer, but it seeks it
    not within itself: it wanders in
    quest of grass.

VII

I. 85. *Sādho, Brahm alakh lakhāyā*

WHEN He Himself reveals Him-
    self, Brahma brings into mani-
    festation That which can never be
    seen.
As the seed is in the plant, as the shade
    is in the tree, as the void is in the
    sky, as infinite forms are in the
    void —
So from beyond the Infinite, the Infi-
    nite comes; and from the Infinite
    the finite extends.

The creature is in Brahma, and Brahma
    is in the creature: they are ever
    distinct, yet ever united.
He Himself is the tree, the seed, and
    the germ.

He Himself is the flower, the fruit, and
the shade.
He Himself is the sun, the light, and
the lighted.
He Himself is Brahma, creature, and
Maya.
He Himself is the manifold form, the
infinite space;
He is the breath, the word, and the
meaning.
He Himself is the limit and the limit-
less: and beyond both the limited
and the limitless is He, the Pure
Being.
He is the Immanent Mind in Brahma
and in the creature.

The Supreme Soul is seen within the
soul,
The Point is seen within the Supreme
Soul,
And within the Point, the reflection is
seen again.

Kabir is blest because he has this
supreme vision !

VIII

I. 101. *is ghaṭ antar bāg bagīce*

WITHIN this earthen vessel are
bowers and groves, and within
it is the Creator :

Within this vessel are the seven oceans
and the unnumbered stars.

The touchstone and the jewel-ap-
praiser are within ;

And within this vessel the Eternal
soundeth, and the spring wells up.

Kabir says : "Listen to me, my Friend !
My beloved Lord is within."

IX

I. 104. *aisā lo nahīn taisā lo*

O HOW may I ever express that
secret word ?

O how can I say He is not like this, and
He is like that ?

If I say that He is within me, the universe is ashamed:

If I say that He is without me, it is falsehood.

He makes the inner and the outer worlds to be indivisibly one;

The conscious and the unconscious, both are His footstools.

He is neither manifest nor hidden, He is neither revealed nor unrevealed:

There are no words to tell that which He is.

X

I. 121. *tohi mori lagan lagāye re phakīr wā*

TO Thee Thou hast drawn my love, O Fakir!

I was sleeping in my own chamber, and Thou didst awaken me; striking me with Thy voice, O Fakir!

I was drowning in the deeps of the

ocean of this world, and Thou
didst save me: upholding me
with Thine arm, O Fakir!

Only one word and no second — and
Thou hast made me tear off all
my bonds, O Fakir!

Kabir says, "Thou hast united Thy
heart to my heart, O Fakir!"

XI

I. 131.   *niś din khelat rahī sakhiyān*
sang

I PLAYED day and night with my
comrades, and now I am greatly
afraid.

So high is my Lord's palace, my heart
trembles to mount its stairs: yet
I must not be shy, if I would enjoy
His love.

My heart must cleave to my Lover;
I must withdraw my veil, and
meet Him with all my body:

Mine eyes must perform the ceremony
  of the lamps of love.
Kabir says: "Listen to me, friend: he
  understands who loves. If you
  feel not love's longing for your
  Beloved One, it is vain to adorn
  your body, vain to put unguent
  on your eyelids."

XII

II. 24. *haṃsā, kaho purātan vāt*

TELL me, O Swan, your ancient
  tale.
From what land do you come, O Swan?
  to what shore will you fly?
Where would you take your rest, O
  Swan, and what do you seek?

Even this morning, O Swan, awake,
  arise, follow me!
There is a land where no doubt nor
  sorrow have rule: where the terror
  of Death is no more.

There the woods of spring are a-bloom,
　　and the fragrant scent "He is I"
　　is borne on the wind:
There the bee of the heart is deeply
　　immersed, and desires no other joy.

XIII

II. 37. *aṅgaḍhiyā devā*

O LORD Increate, who will serve
　　Thee?
Every votary offers his worship to the
　　God of his own creation: each day
　　he receives service —
None seek Him, the Perfect: Brahma,
　　the Indivisible Lord.
They believe in ten Avatars; but no
　　Avatar can be the Infinite Spirit,
　　for he suffers the results of his
　　deeds:
The Supreme One must be other than
　　this.
The Yogi, the Sanyasi, the Ascetics,
　　are disputing one with another:

Kabir says, "O brother! he who has seen that radiance of love, he is saved."

XIV

II. 56.   *dariyā kī lahar dariyāo hai jī*

THE river and its waves are one surf: where is the difference between the river and its waves?

When the wave rises, it is the water; and when it falls, it is the same water again.   Tell me, Sir, where is the distinction?

Because it has been named as wave, shall it no longer be considered as water?

Within the Supreme Brahma, the worlds are being told like beads: Look upon that rosary with the eyes of wisdom.

XV

II. 57.   *jānh khelat vasant ṛiturāj*

WHERE Spring, the lord of the
        seasons, reigneth, there the
Unstruck Music sounds of itself,
There the streams of light flow in all
        directions ;
Few are the men who can cross to that
        shore !
There, where millions of Krishnas stand
        with hands folded,
Where millions of Vishnus bow their
        heads,
Where millions of Brahmās are reading
        the Vedas,
Where millions of Shivas are lost in
        contemplation,
Where millions of Indras dwell in the sky,
Where the demi-gods and the munis
        are unnumbered,
Where millions of Saraswatis, Goddess
        of Music, play on the vina —

There is my Lord self-revealed : and
the scent of sandal and flowers
dwells in those deeps.

XVI

II. 59. *jānh cet acet khambh dōū*

BETWEEN the poles of the conscious and the unconscious, there
has the mind made a swing :

Thereon hang all beings and all worlds,
and that swing never ceases its
sway.

Millions of beings are there : the sun
and the moon in their courses are
there :

Millions of ages pass, and the swing
goes on.

All swing ! the sky and the earth and
the air and the water ; and the
Lord Himself taking form :

And the sight of this has made Kabir
a servant.

XVII

II. 61. *grah candra tapan jot varat hai*

THE light of the sun, the moon, and
the stars shines bright:

The melody of love swells forth, and
the rhythm of love's detachment
beats the time.

Day and night, the chorus of music fills
the heavens; and Kabir says

"My Beloved One gleams like the
lightning flash in the sky."

Do you know how the moments perform their adoration?

Waving its row of lamps, the universe
sings in worship day and night,

There are the hidden banner and the
secret canopy:

There the sound of the unseen bells is
heard.

Kabir says: "There adoration never
ceases; there the Lord of the Universe sitteth on His throne."

The whole world does its works and
commits its errors : but few are
the lovers who know the Beloved.
The devout seeker is he who mingles
in his heart the double currents of
love and detachment, like the
mingling of the streams of Ganges
and Jumna ;
In his heart the sacred water flows day
and night ; and thus the round of
births and deaths is brought to an
end.

Behold what wonderful rest is in the
Supreme Spirit ! and he enjoys it,
who makes himself meet for it.
Held by the cords of love, the swing of
the Ocean of Joy sways to and fro ;
and a mighty sound breaks forth
in song.
See what a lotus blooms there without
water ! and Kabir says
"My heart's bee drinks its nectar."

What a wonderful lotus it is, that
    blooms at the heart of the spinning
    wheel of the universe! Only a
    few pure souls know of its true
    delight.
Music is all around it, and there the
    heart partakes of the joy of the
    Infinite Sea.
Kabir says: "Dive thou into that
    Ocean of sweetness: thus let all
    errors of life and of death flee
    away."

Behold how the thirst of the five senses
    is quenched there! and the three
    forms of misery are no more!
Kabir says: "It is the sport of the
    Unattainable One: look within,
    and behold how the moon-beams
    of that Hidden One shine in you."

There falls the rhythmic beat of life
    and death:

Rapture wells forth, and all space is
  radiant with light.
There the Unstruck Music is sounded;
  it is the music of the love of the
  three worlds.
There millions of lamps of sun and of
  moon are burning;
There the drum beats, and the lover
  swings in play.
There love-songs resound, and light
  rains in showers; and the worshipper is entranced in the taste
  of the heavenly nectar.
Look upon life and death; there is no
  separation between them,
The right hand and the left hand are
  one and the same.
Kabir says: "There the wise man is
  speechless; for this truth may never
  be found in Vadas or in books."

I have had my Seat on the Self-poised
  One,

I have drunk of the Cup of the Ineffable,

I have found the Key of the Mystery,

I have reached the Root of Union.

Travelling by no track, I have come to the Sorrowless Land: very easily has the mercy of the great Lord come upon me.

They have sung of Him as infinite and unattainable: but I in my meditations have seen Him without sight.

That is indeed the sorrowless land, and none know the path that leads there:

Only he who is on that path has surely transcended all sorrow.

Wonderful is that land of rest, to which no merit can win;

It is the wise who has seen it, it is the wise who has sung of it.

This is the Ultimate Word: but can any express its marvellous savour?

He who has savoured it once, he
    knows what joy it can give.
Kabir says: "Knowing it, the ignorant
    man becomes wise, and the wise
    man becomes speechless and silent,
The worshipper is utterly inebriated,
His wisdom and his detachment are
    made perfect;
He drinks from the cup of the in-
    breathings and the outbreathings
    of love."

There the whole sky is filled with
    sound, and there that music is
    made without fingers and without
    strings;
There the game of pleasure and pain
    does not cease.
Kabir says: "If you merge your life
    in the Ocean of Life, you will find
    your life in the Supreme Land of
    Bliss."

What a frenzy of ecstasy there is in

every hour! and the worshipper is
pressing out and drinking the
essence of the hours: he lives in
the life of Brahma.

I speak truth, for I have accepted truth
in life; I am now attached to
truth, I have swept all tinsel away.

Kabir says: "Thus is the worshipper
set free from fear; thus have all
errors of life and of death left
him."

There the sky is filled with music:

There it rains nectar:

There the harp-strings jingle, and there
the drums beat.

What a secret splendour is there, in
the mansion of the sky!

There no mention is made of the rising
and the setting of the sun;

In the ocean of manifestation, which is
the light of love, day and night
are felt to be one.

Joy for ever, no sorrow, no struggle!
There have I seen joy filled to the brim,
    perfection of joy;
No place for error is there.
Kabir says: "There have I witnessed
    the sport of One Bliss!"

I have known in my body the sport of
    the universe: I have escaped from
    the error of this world.
The inward and the outward are be-
    come as one sky, the Infinite and
    the finite are united: I am drunken
    with the sight of this All!
This Light of Thine fulfils the uni-
    verse: the lamp of love that burns
    on the salver of knowledge.
Kabir says: "There error cannot enter,
    and the conflict of life and death
    is felt no more."

XVIII

II. 77.   *maddh ākās āp jahān baiṭhe*

THE middle region of the sky,
    wherein the spirit dwelleth, is
    radiant with the music of light;

There, where the pure and white music
    blossoms, my Lord takes His de-
    light.

In the wondrous effulgence of each hair
    of His body, the brightness of mill-
    ions of suns and of moons is lost.

On that shore there is a city, where the
    rain of nectar pours and pours, and
    never ceases.

Kabir says: "Come, O Dharmadas!
    and see my great Lord's Durbar."

XIX

II. 20.   *paramātam guru nikaṭ virājain*

O MY heart! the Supreme Spirit,
    the great Master, is near you:
    wake, oh wake!

Run to the feet of your Beloved: for

your Lord stands near to your
head.
You have slept for unnumbered ages;
this morning will you not wake?

XX

II. 22.   *man tu pār utar kānh jaiho*

TO what shore would you cross, O
my heart? there is no traveller
before you, there is no road:
Where is the movement, where is the
rest, on that shore?
There is no water; no boat, no boat-
man, is there;
There is not so much as a rope to tow
the boat, nor a man to draw it.
No earth, no sky, no time, no thing, is
there: no shore, no ford!
There, there is neither body nor mind:
and where is the place that shall
still the thirst of the soul? You
shall find naught in that emptiness.
Be strong, and enter into your own

body: for there your foothold is
firm. Consider it well, O my
heart! go not elsewhere.

Kabir says: "Put all imaginations
away, and stand fast in that which
you are."

XXI

II. 33.   *ghar ghar dīpak barai*

LAMPS burn in every house, O
blind one! and you cannot see
them.

One day your eyes shall suddenly be
opened, and you shall see: and the
fetters of death will fall from you.

There is nothing to say or to hear,
there is nothing to do: it is he
who is living, yet dead, who shall
never die again.

Because he lives in solitude, therefore
the Yogi says that his home is far
away.

Your Lord is near: yet you are climbing the palm-tree to seek Him.

The Brahman priest goes from house to house and initiates people into faith:

Alas! the true fountain of life is beside you, and you have set up a stone to worship.

Kabir says: "I may never express how sweet my Lord is. Yoga and the telling of beads, virtue and vice — these are naught to Him."

XXII

II. 38. *Sādho, so satgur mohi bhāwai*

O BROTHER, my heart yearns for that true Guru, who fills the cup of true love, and drinks of it himself, and offers it then to me.

He removes the veil from the eyes, and gives the true Vision of Brahma:

He reveals the worlds in Him, and

makes me to hear the Unstruck
Music:
He shows joy and sorrow to be one:
He fills all utterance with love.
Kabir says: "Verily he has no fear,
who has such a Guru to lead him
to the shelter of safety!"

XXIII

II. 40.   *tinwir sāñjh kā gahirā āwai*

THE shadows of evening fall thick
and deep, and the darkness of love
envelops the body and the mind.
Open the window to the west, and be
lost in the sky of love;
Drink the sweet honey that steeps the
petals of the lotus of the heart.
Receive the waves in your body: what
splendour is in the region of the
sea!
Hark! the sounds of conches and bells
are rising.

Kabir says: "O brother, behold! the
Lord is in this vessel of my body."

XXIV

II. 48. *jis se rahani apār jagat men*

MORE than all else do I cherish at
heart that love which makes
me to live a limitless life in this
world.

It is like the lotus, which lives in the
water and blooms in the water:
yet the water cannot touch its
petals, they open beyond its reach.

It is like a wife, who enters the fire at
the bidding of love. She burns
and lets others grieve, yet never
dishonours love.

This ocean of the world is hard to cross:
its waters are very deep. Kabir
says: "Listen to me, O Sadhu!
few there are who have reached its
end."

XXV

II. 45. *Hari ne apnā āp chipāyā*

MY Lord hides Himself, and my
Lord wonderfully reveals Himself:

My Lord has encompassed me with
hardness, and my Lord has cast
down my limitations.

My Lord brings to me words of sorrow
and words of joy, and He Himself
heals their strife.

I will offer my body and mind to my
Lord: I will give up my life, but
never can I forget my Lord!

XXVI

II. 75. *ōnkār siwae kōī sirjai*

ALL things are created by the Om;
The love-form is His body.

He is without form, without quality,
without decay:

Seek thou union with Him!

But that formless God takes a thousand
      forms in the eyes of His creatures:
He is pure and indestructible,
His form is infinite and fathomless,
He dances in rapture, and waves of
      form arise from His dance.
The body and the mind cannot contain
      themselves, when they are touched
      by His great joy.
He is immersed in all consciousness, all
      joys, and all sorrows;
He has no beginning and no end;
He holds all within His bliss.

XXVII

II. 81.   *satgur sōī dayā kar dīnhā*

IT is the mercy of my true Guru that
    has made me to know the un-
    known;
I have learned from Him how to walk
      without feet, to see without eyes,
      to hear without ears, to drink

without mouth, to fly without
wings;

I have brought my love and my meditation into the land where there
is no sun and moon, nor day and
night.

Without eating, I have tasted of the
sweetness of nectar; and without
water, I have quenched my thirst.

Where there is the response of delight,
there is the fullness of joy. Before whom can that joy be uttered?

Kabir says: "The Guru is great beyond words, and great is the good
fortune of the disciple."

XXVIII

II. 85. *nirguṇ āge sarguṇ nācai*

BEFORE the Unconditioned, the
Conditioned dances:

"Thou and I are one!" this trumpet
proclaims.

The Guru comes, and bows down before
    the disciple:
This is the greatest of wonders.

XXIX

II. 87. *Kabīr kab se bhaye vairāgī*

GORAKHNATH asks Kabir:
    "Tell me, O Kabir, when did
    your vocation begin? Where did
    your love have its rise?"
Kabir answers:
"When He whose forms are manifold
    had not begun His play: when
    there was no Guru, and no disciple:
    when the world was not spread
    out: when the Supreme One was
    alone —
Then I became an ascetic; then, O
    Gorakh, my love was drawn to
    Brahma.
Brahmā did not hold the crown on his
    head; the god Vishnu was not

anointed as king; the power of
Shiva was still unborn; when I
was instructed in Yoga.

I became suddenly revealed in Benares,
and Ramananda illumined me;
I brought with me the thirst for the
Infinite, and I have come for the
meeting with Him.
In simplicity will I unite with the
Simple One; my love will surge
up.
O Gorakh, march thou with His
music!"

XXX

II. 95.   *yā tarvar men ek pakherū*

ON this tree is a bird: it dances
in the joy of life.
None knows where it is: and who
knows what the burden of its
music may be?
Where the branches throw a deep

shade, there does it have its nest:
and it comes in the evening and
flies away in the morning, and says
not a word of that which it means.
None tell me of this bird that sings
within me.
It is neither coloured nor colourless: it
has neither form nor outline:
It sits in the shadow of love.
It dwells within the Unattainable, the
Infinite, and the Eternal; and no
one marks when it comes and goes.
Kabir says: "O brother Sadhu! deep
is the mystery.   Let wise men seek
to know where rests that bird."

XXXI

II. 100.   *niś din sālai ghāw*

A SORE pain troubles me day and
night, and I cannot sleep;
I long for the meeting with my Beloved,
and my father's house gives me
pleasure no more.

The gates of the sky are opened, the
     temple is revealed :
I meet my husband, and leave at His
     feet the offering of my body and
     my mind.

XXXII

II. 103.   *nāco re mero man, matta hoy*

DANCE, my heart! dance to-day
     with joy.
The strains of love fill the days and
     the nights with music, and the
     world is listening to its melodies :
Mad with joy, life and death dance to
     the rhythm of this music.   The
     hills and the sea and the earth
     dance.   The world of man dances
     in laughter and tears.
Why put on the robe of the monk, and
     live aloof from the world in lonely
     pride ?
Behold ! my heart dances in the de-

light of a hundred arts; and the
Creator is well pleased.

XXXIII

II. 105. *man mast huā tab kyon bole*

WHERE is the need of words,
when love has made drunken
the heart?
I have wrapped the diamond in my
cloak; why open it again and
again?
When its load was light, the pan of the
balance went up: now it is full,
where is the need for weighing?
The swan has taken its flight to the
lake beyond the mountains; why
should it search for the pools and
ditches any more?
Your Lord dwells within you: why
need your outward eyes be opened?
Kabir says: "Listen, my brother! my
Lord, who ravishes my eyes, has
united Himself with me."

XXXIV

II. 110. *mohi tohi lāgī kaise chuṭe*

HOW could the love between Thee
and me sever?

As the leaf of the lotus abides on the
water: so thou art my Lord, and
I am Thy servant.

As the night-bird Chakor gazes all
night at the moon: so Thou art
my Lord and I am Thy servant.

From the beginning until the ending
of time, there is love between
Thee and me; and how shall such
love be extinguished?

Kabir says: "As the river enters into the
ocean, so my heart touches Thee."

XXXV

II. 113. *vālam, āwo hamāre geh re*

MY body and my mind are grieved
for the want of Thee;

O my Beloved! come to my house.

When people say I am Thy bride, I am
    ashamed; for I have not touched
    Thy heart with my heart.

Then what is this love of mine? I have
    no taste for food, I have no sleep;
    my heart is ever restless within
    doors and without.

As water is to the thirsty, so is the
    lover to the bride. Who is there
    that will carry my news to my
    Beloved?

Kabir is restless: he is dying for sight
    of Him.

XXXVI

II. 126. *jāg piyārī, ab kān sowai*

O FRIEND, awake, and sleep no
    more!

The night is over and gone, would you
    lose your day also?

Others, who have wakened, have re-
    ceived jewels;

O foolish woman! you have lost all
    whilst you slept.

Your lover is wise, and you are foolish,
    O woman!

You never prepared the bed of your
    husband:

O mad one! you passed your time in
    silly play.

Your youth was passed in vain, for you
    did not know your Lord;

Wake, wake! See! your bed is empty:
    He left you in the night.

Kabir says: "Only she wakes, whose
    heart is pierced with the arrow
    of His music."

XXXVII

I. 36.   *sūr parkās, tanh rain kahān*
            pāïye

WHERE is the night, when the
    sun is shining? If it is night,
then the sun withdraws its light.

Where knowledge is, can ignorance en-

dure? If there be ignorance, then
knowledge must die.
If there be lust, how can love be there?
Where there is love, there is no lust.

Lay hold on your sword, and join in
the fight. Fight, O my brother,
as long as life lasts.
Strike off your enemy's head, and
there make an end of him quickly:
then come, and bow your head at
your King's Durbar.
He who is brave, never forsakes the
battle: he who flies from it is no
true fighter.
In the field of this body a great war
goes forward, against passion, anger, pride, and greed:
It is in the kingdom of truth, content-
ment and purity, that this battle
is raging; and the sword that
rings forth most loudly is the
sword of His Name.

Kabir says: "When a brave knight
takes the field, a host of cowards
is put to flight.

It is a hard fight and a weary one, this
fight of the truth-seeker: for the
vow of the truth-seeker is more
hard than that of the warrior,
or of the widowed wife who would
follow her husband.

For the warrior fights for a few hours,
and the widow's struggle with
death is soon ended:

But the truth-seeker's battle goes on
day and night, as long as life lasts
it never ceases."

XXXVIII

I. 50. *bhram kā tālā lagā mahal re*

THE lock of error shuts the gate,
open it with the key of love:
Thus, by opening the door, thou shalt
wake the Beloved.

Kabir says: "O brother! do not pass
by such good fortune as this."

XXXIX

I. 59. *sādho, yah tan ṭhāṭh tanvure kā*

O FRIEND! this body is His lyre;
He tightens its strings, and draws
from it the melody of Brahma.

If the strings snap and the keys
slacken, then to dust must this in-
strument of dust return:

Kabir says: "None but Brahma can
evoke its melodies."

XL

I. 65. *avadhū bhūle ko ghar lāwe*

HE is dear to me indeed who can
call back the wanderer to his
home. In the home is the true
union, in the home is enjoyment of
life: why should I forsake my
home and wander in the forest?

If Brahma helps me to realize
truth, verily I will find both bondage and deliverance in home.

He is dear to me indeed who has power
to dive deep into Brahma; whose
mind loses itself with ease in His
contemplation.

He is dear to me who knows Brahma,
and can dwell on His supreme
truth in meditation; and who can
play the melody of the Infinite by
uniting love and renunciation in life.

Kabir says: "The home is the abiding
place; in the home is reality; the
home helps to attain Him Who is
real. So stay where you are, and all
things shall come to you in time.'

XLI

I. 76.   *santo, sahaj samādh bhalī*

O SADHU! the simple union is the
best.

Since the day when I met with my

Lord, there has been no end to
the sport of our love.
I shut not my eyes, I close not my ears,
I do not mortify my body;
I see with eyes open and smile, and
behold His beauty everywhere:
I utter His Name, and whatever I see,
it reminds me of Him; whatever
I do, it becomes His worship.
The rising and the setting are one to
me; all contradictions are solved.
Wherever I go, I move round Him,
All I achieve is His service:
When I lie down, I lie prostrate at His
feet.

He is the only adorable one to me: I
have none other.
My tongue has left off impure words,
it sings His glory day and night:
Whether I rise or sit down, I can never
forget Him; for the rhythm of
His music beats in my ears.

Kabir says: "My heart is frenzied, and I disclose in my soul what is hidden. I am immersed in that one great bliss which transcends all pleasure and pain."

XLII

I. 79. *tīrath men to sab pānī hai*

THERE is nothing but water at the holy bathing places; and I know that they are useless, for I have bathed in them.

The images are all lifeless, they cannot speak; I know, for I have cried aloud to them.

The Purana and the Koran are mere words; lifting up the curtain, I have seen.

Kabir gives utterance to the words of experience; and he knows very well that all other things are untrue.

XLIII

I. 82.   *pānī vic mīn piyāsī*

I LAUGH when I hear that the fish
  in the water is thirsty:
You do not see that the Real is in your
    home, and you wander from forest
    to forest listlessly!
Here is the truth!   Go where you will,
    to Benares or to Mathura; if you
    do not find your soul, the world is
    unreal to you.

XLIV

I. 93.   *gagan maṭh gaib nisān gaḍe*

THE Hidden Banner is planted in
  the temple of the sky; there the
    blue canopy decked with the moon
    and set with bright jewels is spread.
There the light of the sun and the
    moon is shining: still your mind
    to silence before that splendour.

Kabir says: "He who has drunk of this
    nectar, wanders like one who is
    mad."

XLV

I. 97. *sādho, ko hai kānh se āyo*

WHO are you, and whence do you
    come?
Where dwells that Supreme Spirit, and
    how does He have His sport with
    all created things?
The fire is in the wood; but who
    awakens it suddenly? Then it
    turns to ashes, and where goes the
    force of the fire?
The true guru teaches that He has
    neither limit nor infinitude.
Kabir says: "Brahma suits His lan-
    guage to the understanding of His
    hearer."

XLVI

I. 98. *sādho, sahajai kāyā śodho*

O SADHU! purify your body in
the simple way.

As the seed is within the banyan tree,
and within the seed are the flowers,
the fruits, and the shade:

So the germ is within the body, and
within that germ is the body again.

The fire, the air, the water, the earth,
and the aether; you cannot have
these outside of Him.

O Kazi, O Pundit, consider it well:
what is there that is not in the
soul?

The water-filled pitcher is placed upon
water, it has water within and
without.

It should not be given a name, lest it
call forth the error of dualism.

Kabir says: "Listen to the Word, the
Truth, which is your essence. He

speaks the Word to Himself; and
He Himself is the Creator."

XLVII

I. 102. *tarvar ek mūl vin ṭhāḍā*

THERE is a strange tree, which
stands without roots and bears
fruits without blossoming;
It has no branches and no leaves, it is
lotus all over.
Two birds sing there; one is the Guru,
and the other the disciple:
The disciple chooses the manifold fruits
of life and tastes them, and the
Guru beholds him in joy.
What Kabir says is hard to understand:
" The bird is beyond seeking, yet it
is most clearly visible.   The Formless is in the midst of all forms.   I
sing the glory of forms."

XLVIII

I. 107.   *calat mansā acal kīnhī*

I HAVE stilled my restless mind, and
my heart is radiant: for in That-
ness I have seen beyond That-ness,
in company I have seen the Comrade Himself.

Living in bondage, I have set myself
free: I have broken away from
the clutch of all narrowness.

Kabir says: "I have attained the
unattainable, and my heart is
coloured with the colour of love."

XLIX

I. 105.   *jo dīsai, so to hai nāhīn*

THAT which you see is not: and for
that which is, you have no words.

Unless you see, you believe not: what
is told you you cannot accept.

He who is discerning knows by the word;
and the ignorant stands gaping.

Some contemplate the Formless, and
others meditate on form: but the
wise man knows that Brahma is
beyond both.

That beauty of His is not seen of the
eye: that metre of His is not heard
of the ear.

Kabir says: "He who has found both
love and renunciation never descends to death."

L

I. 126. *murali bajat akhaṇḍ sadāye*

THE flute of the Infinite is played
without ceasing, and its sound is
love:

When love renounces all limits, it
reaches truth.

How widely the fragrance spreads! It
has no end, nothing stands in its
way.

The form of this melody is bright like

a million suns: incomparably
sounds the vina, the vina of the
notes of truth.

LI

I. 129. *sakhiyo, ham hūn bhāī vāla-
mā́sī*

DEAR friend, I am eager to meet
my Beloved! My youth has
flowered, and the pain of separation from Him troubles my breast.
I am wandering yet in the alleys of
knowledge without purpose, but I
have received His news in these
alleys of knowledge.
I have a letter from my Beloved: in
this letter is an unutterable mes-
sage, and now my fear of death is
done away.
Kabir says: "O my loving friend! I
have got for my gift the Deathless
One."

LII

I. 130.   *sāin̄ vin dard kareje hoy*

WHEN I am parted from my
    Beloved, my heart is full of
misery: I have no comfort in the
day, I have no sleep in the night.
To whom shall I tell my sorrow?
The night is dark; the hours slip by.
    Because my Lord is absent, I start
    up and tremble with fear.
Kabir says: "Listen, my friend! there
    is no other satisfaction, save in the
    encounter with the Beloved."

LIII

I. 122.   *kaum muralī śabd śun ānand
            bhayo*

WHAT is that flute whose music
    thrills me with joy?
The flame burns without a lamp;
The lotus blossoms without a root;

Flowers bloom in clusters;
The moon-bird is devoted to the moon;
With all its heart the rain-bird longs
    for the shower of rain;
But upon whose love does the Lover
    concentrate His entire life?

LIV

I. 112. *śuntā nahī dhun kī khabar*

HAVE you not heard the tune
which the Unstruck Music is
playing? In the midst of the
chamber the harp of joy is gently
and sweetly played; and where is
the need of going without to hear
it?

If you have not drunk of the nectar of
that One Love, what boots it
though you should purge yourself
of all stains?

The Kazi is searching the words of the
Koran, and instructing others:

but if his heart be not steeped in
that love, what does it avail,
though he be a teacher of men?

The Yogi dyes his garments with red:
but if he knows naught of that
colour of love, what does it avail
though his garments be tinted?

Kabir says: "Whether I be in the
temple or the balcony, in the camp
or in the flower garden, I tell you
truly that every moment my Lord
is taking His delight in me."

LV

I. 73.   bhakti kā mārag jhīnā re

SUBTLE is the path of love!
   Therein there is no asking and
no not-asking,

There one loses one's self at His feet,

There one is immersed in the joy of
the seeking: plunged in the deeps
of love as the fish in the water.

The lover is never slow in offering his
     head for his Lord's service.
Kabir declares the secret of this love.

LVI

I. 68.   *bhāī kōī satguru sant kahāwai*

HE is the real Sadhu, who can re-
     veal the form of the Formless to
     the vision of these eyes:
Who teaches the simple way of attain-
     ing Him, that is other than rites
     or ceremonies:
Who does not make you close the doors,
     and hold the breath, and renounce
     the world:
Who makes you perceive the Supreme
     Spirit wherever the mind attaches
     itself:
Who teaches you to be still in the midst
     of all your activities.
Ever immersed in bliss, having no fear
     in his mind, he keeps the spirit of

union in the midst of all enjoyments.

The infinite dwelling of the Infinite Being is everywhere: in earth, water, sky, and air:

Firm as the thunderbolt, the seat of the seeker is established above the void.

He who is within is without: I see Him and none else.

LVII

I. 66.   *sādho, śabd sādhnā kījai*

RECEIVE that Word from which the Universe springeth!

That word is the Guru; I have heard it, and become the disciple.

How many are there who know the meaning of that word?

O Sadhu! practise that Word!

The Vedas and the Puranas proclaim it,

The world is established in it,

The Rishis and devotees speak of it:
But none knows the mystery of the
    Word.
The householder leaves his house when
    he hears it,
The ascetic comes back to love when
    he hears it,
The Six Philosophies expound it,
The Spirit of Renunciation points to
    that Word,
From that Word the world-form has
    sprung,
That Word reveals all.
Kabir says: "But who knows whence
    the Word cometh?"

LVIII

I. 63. *pīle pyālā, ho matwālā*

EMPTY the Cup! O be drunken!
    Drink the divine nectar of His
Name!
Kabir says: "Listen to me, dear Sadhu!

From the sole of the foot to the crown
of the head this mind is filled with
poison."

LIX

I. 52.   *khasm na cīnhai bāwarī*

O MAN, if thou dost not know thine
own Lord, whereof art thou so
proud?
Put thy cleverness away: mere words
shall never unite thee to Him.
Do not deceive thyself with the witness
of the Scriptures:
Love is something other than this, and
he who has sought it truly has
found it.

LX

I. 56.   *sukh sindh kī sair kā*

THE savour of wandering in the
ocean of deathless life has rid
me of all my asking:

As the tree is in the seed, so all diseases
are in this asking.

LXI

I. 48.   *sukh sāgar men āīke*

WHEN at last you are come to the
ocean of happiness, do not go
back thirsty.

Wake, foolish man! for Death stalks
you.   Here is pure water before
you; drink it at every breath.

Do not follow the mirage on foot, but
thirst for the nectar;

Dhruva, Prahlad, and Shukadeva have
drunk of it, and also Raidas has
tasted it:

The saints are drunk with love, their
thirst is for love.

Kabir says: "Listen to me, brother!
The nest of fear is broken.

Not for a moment have you come face
to face with the world:

You are weaving your bondage of falsehood, your words are full of deception :

With the load of desires which you hold on your head, how can you be light ? "

Kabir says : "Keep within you truth, detachment, and love."

LXII

I. 35.   *satī ko kaun śikhāwtā hai*

WHO has ever taught the widowed wife to burn herself on the pyre of her dead husband ?

And who has ever taught love to find bliss in renunciation ?

LXIII

I. 39.   *are man, dhīraj kāhe na dharai*

WHY so impatient, my heart ?
He who watches over birds, beasts, and insects,

He who cared for you whilst you were
yet in your mother's womb,
Shall He not care for you now that you
are come forth?
Oh my heart, how could you turn from
the smile of your Lord and wander
so far from Him?
You have left your Beloved and are
thinking of others: and this is
why all your work is in vain.

LXIV

I. 117. *sāin̲ se lagan kaṭhin hai, bhāī*

HOW hard it is to meet my Lord!
The rain-bird wails in thirst for
the rain: almost she dies of her
longing, yet she would have none
other water than the rain.
Drawn by the love of music, the deer
moves forward: she dies as she
listens to the music, yet she shrinks
not in fear.

The widowed wife sits by the body of
   her dead husband: she is not
   afraid of the fire.
Put away all fear for this poor body.

LXV

I. 22.   jab main bhūlā, re bhāī

O BROTHER! when I was for-
   getful, my true Guru showed me
the Way.
Then I left off all rites and ceremonies,
   I bathed no more in the holy
   water:
Then I learned that it was I alone who
   was mad, and the whole world
   beside me was sane; and I had
   disturbed these wise people.
From that time forth I knew no more
   how to roll in the dust in obei-
   sance:
I do not ring the temple bell:
I do not set the idol on its throne:

I do not worship the image with flowers.
It is not the austerities that mortify the
  flesh which are pleasing to the Lord,
When you leave off your clothes and
  kill your senses, you do not please
  the Lord:
The man who is kind and who practises
  righteousness, who remains passive
  amidst the affairs of the world,
  who considers all creatures on
  earth as his own self,
He attains the Immortal Being, the
  true God is ever with him.
Kabir says: "He attains the true
  Name whose words are pure, and
  who is free from pride and con-
  ceit."

LXVI

I. 20.   *man na raṅgāye*

THE Yogi dyes his garments, in-
  stead of dyeing his mind in the
colours of love:

He sits within the temple of the Lord,
leaving Brahma to worship a stone.

He pierces holes in his ears, he has a
great beard and matted locks, he
looks like a goat:

He goes forth into the wilderness, kill-
ing all his desires, and turns himself into an eunuch:

He shaves his head and dyes his garments; he reads the Gita and becomes a mighty talker.

Kabir says: "You are going to the
doors of death, bound hand and
foot!"

LXVII

I. 9. *nā jāne sāhab kaisā hai*

I DO not know what manner of God
is mine.

The Mullah cries aloud to Him: and
why? Is your Lord deaf? The
subtle anklets that ring on the

feet of an insect when it moves
are heard of Him.

Tell your beads, paint your forehead
with the mark of your God, and
wear matted locks long and showy:
but a deadly weapon is in your
heart, and how shall you have
God?

LXVIII

III. 102. *ham se rahā na jāy*

I HEAR the melody of His flute, and
I cannot contain myself:

The flower blooms, though it is not
spring; and already the bee has
received its invitation.

The sky roars and the lightning flashes,
the waves arise in my heart,

The rain falls; and my heart longs for
my Lord.

Where the rhythm of the world rises
and falls, thither my heart has
reached:

There the hidden banners are fluttering
    in the air.
Kabir says: "My heart is dying,
    though it lives."

LXIX

III. 2. *jo khodā masjid vasat hai*

IF God be within the mosque, then
    to whom does this world belong?
If Ram be within the image which you
    find upon your pilgrimage, then
    who is there to know what happens
    without?
Hari is in the East: Allah is in the
    West. Look within your heart,
    for there you will find both Karim
    and Ram;
All the men and women of the world
    are His living forms.
Kabir is the child of Allah and of Ram:
    He is my Guru, He is my Pir.

LXX

III. 9.   *śīl santosh sadā samadṛishṭi*

HE who is meek and contented, he who has an equal vision, whose mind is filled with the fullness of acceptance and of rest;

He who has seen Him and touched Him, he is freed from all fear and trouble.

To him the perpetual thought of God is like sandal paste smeared on the body, to him nothing else is delight:

His work and his rest are filled with music: he sheds abroad the radiance of love.

Kabir says: "Touch His feet, who is one and indivisible, immutable and peaceful; who fills all vessels to the brim with joy, and whose form is love."

LXXI

III. 13.   *sādh saṅgat pītam*

GO thou to the company of the good, where the Beloved One has His dwelling place:

Take all thy thoughts and love and instruction from thence.

Let that assembly be burnt to ashes where His Name is not spoken!

Tell me, how couldst thou hold a wedding-feast, if the bridegroom himself were not there?

Waver no more, think only of the Beloved;

Set not thy heart on the worship of other gods, there is no worth in the worship of other masters.

Kabir deliberates and says: "Thus thou shalt never find the Beloved!"

LXXII

III. 26.   *tor hīrā hirāilwā kīcaḍ men*

THE jewel is lost in the mud, and
all are seeking for it;
Some look for it in the east, and some
in the west; some in the water
and some amongst stones.
But the servant Kabir has appraised it
at its true value, and has wrapped
it with care in the end of the
mantle of his heart.

LXXIII

III. 26.   *āyau din gaune kā ho*

THE palanquin came to take me
away to my husband's home,
and it sent through my heart a
thrill of joy;
But the bearers have brought me into
the lonely forest, where I have no
one of my own.

O bearers, I entreat you by your feet,
wait but a moment longer: let me
go back to my kinsmen and friends,
and take my leave of them.

The servant Kabir sings: "O Sadhu!
finish your buying and selling,
have done with your good and
your bad: for there are no mar-
kets and no shops in the land to
which you go."

LXXIV

III. 30. *are dil, prem nagar kā ant na
pāyā*

O MY heart! you have not known
all the secrets of this city of
love: in ignorance you came, and
in ignorance you return.

O my friend, what have you done with
this life? You have taken on your
head the burden heavy with stones,
and who is to lighten it for you?

Your Friend stands on the other shore,
  but you never think in your mind
  how you may meet with Him:
The boat is broken, and yet you sit
  ever upon the bank; and thus you
  are beaten to no purpose by the
  waves.
The servant Kabir asks you to consider; who is there that shall be-
  friend you at the last?
You are alone, you have no companion:
  you will suffer the consequences
  of your own deeds.

LXXV

III. 55.   *ved kahe sarguṇ ke āge*

THE Vedas say that the Unconditioned stands beyond the world
  of Conditions.
O woman, what does it avail thee to
  dispute whether He is beyond all
  or in all?

See thou everything as thine own
dwelling place: the mist of pleasure and pain can never spread there.

There Brahma is revealed day and
night: there light is His garment,
light is His seat, light rests on thy
head.

Kabir says: "The Master, who is true,
He is all light."

LXXVI

III. 48. *tū surat nain nihār*

OPEN your eyes of love, and see
Him who pervades this world!
consider it well, and know that
this is your own country.

When you meet the true Guru, He will
awaken your heart;

He will tell you the secret of love and
detachment, and then you will
know indeed that He transcends
this universe.

This world is the City of Truth, its
  maze of paths enchants the heart:
We can reach the goal without crossing
  the road, such is the sport unend-
  ing.
Where the ring of manifold joys ever
  dances about Him, there is the
  sport of Eternal Bliss.
When we know this, then all our re-
  ceiving and renouncing is over;
Thenceforth the heat of having shall
  never scorch us more.

He is the Ultimate Rest unbounded:
He has spread His form of love throughout all the world.
From that Ray which is Truth, streams
  of new forms are perpetually spring-
  ing: and He pervades those forms.
All the gardens and groves and bowers
  are abounding with blossom; and
  the air breaks forth into ripples
  of joy.

There the swan plays a wonderful game,
There the Unstruck Music eddies
     around the Infinite One;
There in the midst the Throne of the
     Unheld is shining, whereon the
     great Being sits —
Millions of suns are shamed by the
     radiance of a single hair of His
     body.
On the harp of the road what true
     melodies are being sounded! and
     its notes pierce the heart:
There the Eternal Fountain is playing
     its endless life-streams of birth
     and death.
They call Him Emptiness who is the
     Truth of truths, in Whom all
     truths are stored!

There within Him creation goes for-
     ward, which is beyond all philoso-
     phy; for philosophy cannot attain
     to Him:

There is an endless world, O my
Brother! and there is the Name-
less Being, of whom naught can
be said.

Only he knows it who has reached that
region: it is other than all that
is heard and said.

No form, no body, no length, no
breadth is seen there: how can I
tell you that which it is?

He comes to the Path of the Infinite
on whom the grace of the Lord
descends: he is freed from births
and deaths who attains to Him.

Kabir says: "It cannot be told by the
words of the mouth, it cannot be
written on paper:

It is like a dumb person who tastes a
sweet thing — how shall it be ex-
plained?"

LXXVII

III. 60.　cal haṃsā wā deś jahān

O MY heart! let us go to that
country where dwells the Beloved, the ravisher of my heart!

There Love is filling her pitcher from
the well, yet she has no rope where-
with to draw water;

There the clouds do not cover the sky,
yet the rain falls down in gentle
showers:

O bodiless one! do not sit on your
doorstep; go forth and bathe
yourself in that rain!

There it is ever moonlight and never
dark; and who speaks of one sun
only? that land is illuminate with
the rays of a million suns.

LXXVIII

III. 63.   *kahain̄ Kabīr, śuno ho sādho*

KABIR says: "O Sadhu! hear my deathless words. If you want your own good, examine and consider them well.

You have estranged yourself from the Creator, of whom you have sprung: you have lost your reason, you have bought death.

All doctrines and all teachings are sprung from Him, from Him they grow: know this for certain, and have no fear.

Hear from me the tidings of this great truth!

Whose name do you sing, and on whom do you meditate? O, come forth from this entanglement!

He dwells at the heart of all things, so why take refuge in empty desolation?

If you place the Guru at a distance
from you, then it is but the distance that you honour:

If indeed the Master be far away, then
who is it else that is creating this
world?

When you think that He is not here,
then you wander further and
further away, and seek Him in
vain with tears.

Where He is far off, there He is unattainable: where He is near, He
is very bliss.

Kabir says: "Lest His servant should
suffer pain He pervades him
through and through."

Know yourself then, O Kabir; for He
is in you from head to foot.

Sing with gladness, and keep your seat
unmoved within your heart.

LXXIX

III. 66. *nā main dharmī nahīn adharmī*

I AM neither pious nor ungodly,
I live neither by law nor by sense,
I am neither a speaker nor hearer,
I am neither a servant nor master,
I am neither bond nor free,
I am neither detached nor attached.
I am far from none: I am near to none.
I shall go neither to hell nor to heaven.
I do all works; yet I am apart from all works.
Few comprehend my meaning: he who can comprehend it, he sits unmoved.
Kabir seeks neither to establish nor to destroy.

LXXX

III. 69.   *satta nām hai sab ten nyārā*

THE true Name is like none other
   name!
The distinction of the Conditioned
   from the Unconditioned is but a
   word:
The Unconditioned is the seed, the
   Conditioned is the flower and the
   fruit.
Knowledge is the branch, and the
   Name is the root.
Look, and see where the root is: happiness shall be yours when you
   come to the root.
The root will lead you to the branch,
   the leaf, the flower, and the fruit:
It is the encounter with the Lord, it is
   the attainment of bliss, it is the
   reconciliation of the Conditioned
   and the Unconditioned.

LXXXI

III. 74. *pratham ek jo āpai āp*

IN the beginning was He alone, sufficient unto Himself: the formless, colourless, and unconditioned Being.

Then was there neither beginning, middle, nor end;

Then were no eyes, no darkness, no light;

Then were no ground, air, nor sky; no fire, water, nor earth; no rivers like the Ganges and the Jumna, no seas, oceans, and waves.

Then was neither vice nor virtue; scriptures there were not, as the Vedas and Puranas, nor as the Koran.

Kabir ponders in his mind and says, "Then was there no activity: the Supreme Being remained merged in the unknown depths of His own self."

The Guru neither eats nor drinks,
  neither lives nor dies:
Neither has He form, line, colour, nor
  vesture.
He who has neither caste nor clan nor
  anything else — how may I de-
  scribe His glory?
He has neither form nor formlessness,
He has no name,
He has neither colour nor colourless-
  ness,
He has no dwelling-place.

LXXXII

III. 76.   *kahain Kabīr vicār ke*

KABIR ponders and says: "He
  who has neither caste nor country, who is formless and without
  quality, fills all space."
The Creator brought into being the
  Game of Joy: and from the word
  Om the Creation sprang.

The earth is His joy; His joy is the
    sky;

His joy is the flashing of the sun and
    the moon;

His joy is the beginning, the middle,
    and the end;

His joy is eyes, darkness, and light.

Oceans and waves are His joy: His
    joy the Sarasvati, the Jumna, and
    the Ganges.

The Guru is One: and life and death,
    union and separation, are all His
    plays of joy!

His play the land and water, the whole
    universe!

His play the earth and the sky!

In play is the Creation spread out, in
    play it is established. The whole
    world, says Kabir, rests in His
    play, yet still the Player remains
    unknown.

LXXXIII

III. 84.   *jhī jhī jantar bājai*

THE harp gives forth murmurous
music; and the dance goes on
without hands and feet.

It is played without fingers, it is heard
without ears: for He is the ear,
and He is the listener.

The gate is locked, but within there is
fragrance: and there the meeting
is seen of none.

The wise shall understand it.

LXXXIV

III. 89.   *mor phakīrwā māṅgi jāy*

THE Beggar goes a-begging, but
I could not even catch sight of
Him:

And what shall I beg of the Beggar?
He gives without my asking.

Kabir says: "I am His own: now let
that befall which may befall!"

LXXXV

III. 90. *naihar se jiyarā phāṭ re*

MY heart cries aloud for the house
of my lover; the open road and
the shelter of a roof are all one to
her who has lost the city of her
husband.

My heart finds no joy in anything: my
mind and my body are distraught.

His palace has a million gates, but there
is a vast ocean between it and me:

How shall I cross it, O friend? for endless is the outstretching of the path.

How wondrously this lyre is wrought!
When its strings are rightly strung,
it maddens the heart: but when
the keys are broken and the strings
are loosened, none regard it more.

I tell my parents with laughter that I
must go to my Lord in the
morning;

They are angry, for they do not want
   me to go, and they say: "She
   thinks she has gained such do-
   minion over her husband that she
   can have whatsoever she wishes;
   and therefore she is impatient to go
   to him."
Dear friend, lift my veil lightly now;
   for this is the night of love.
Kabir says: "Listen to me! My heart
   is eager to meet my lover: I lie
   sleepless upon my bed. Remem-
   ber me early in the morning!"

LXXXVI

III. 96. *jīv mahal men̄ Śiv pahunwā*

SERVE your God, who has come
   into this temple of life!
Do not act the part of a madman, for
   the night is thickening fast.
He has awaited me for countless ages,

for love of me He has lost His
    heart :
Yet I did not know the bliss that was
    so near to me, for my love was not
    yet awake.
But now, my Lover has made known
    to me the meaning of the note that
    struck my ear :
Now, my good fortune is come.
Kabir says : "Behold ! how great is
    my good fortune ! I have received
    the unending caress of my Be-
    loved !"

LXXXVII

I. 71.   *gagan ghaṭā ghaharānī, sādho*

CLOUDS thicken in the sky ! O,
    listen to the deep voice of their
    roaring ;
The rain comes from the east with its
    monotonous murmur.
Take care of the fences and boundaries

of your fields, lest the rains over-
flow them ;
Prepare the soil of deliverance, and let
the creepers of love and renunciation be soaked in this shower.
It is the prudent farmer who will bring
his harvest home; he shall fill
both his vessels, and feed both
the wise men and the saints.

LXXXVIII

III. 118.   *āj din ke main jāun balihārī*

THIS day is dear to me above all
other days, for to-day the Beloved Lord is a guest in my house ;
My chamber and my courtyard are
beautiful with His presence.
My longings sing His Name, and they
are become lost in His great
beauty :
I wash His feet, and I look upon His
Face; and I lay before Him as an

offering my body, my mind, and
all that I have.

What a day of gladness is that day in
which my Beloved, who is my
treasure, comes to my house!

All evils fly from my heart when I see
my Lord.

"My love has touched Him; my heart
is longing for the Name which is
Truth."

Thus sings Kabir, the servant of all
servants.

LXXXIX

I. 100.   *kōī śuntā hai jñānī rāg gagan
men*

IS there any wise man who will listen
to that solemn music which arises
in the sky?

For He, the Source of all music, makes
all vessels full fraught, and rests in
fullness Himself.

He who is in the body is ever athirst,
　　for he pursues that which is in part:
But ever there wells forth deeper and
　　deeper the sound "He is this —
　　this is He"; fusing love and re-
　　nunciation into one.
Kabir says: "O brother! that is the
　　Primal Word."

XC

I. 108. *main kā se būjhaun*

TO whom shall I go to learn about
　　my Beloved?
Kabir says: "As you never may find
　　the forest if you ignore the tree, so
　　He may never be found in abstrac-
　　tions."

XCI

III. 12. *saṃskirit bhāshā padhi līnhā*

I HAVE learned the Sanskrit lan-
　　guage, so let all men call me wise:
But where is the use of this, when I

am floating adrift, and parched
with thirst, and burning with the
heat of desire?

To no purpose do you bear on your
head this load of pride and vanity.

Kabir says: "Lay it down in the dust,
and go forth to meet the Beloved.
Address Him as your Lord."

XCII

III. 110.   *carkhā calai surat virahin kā*

THE woman who is parted from her
lover spins at the spinning wheel.

The city of the body arises in its
beauty; and within it the palace
of the mind has been built.

The wheel of love revolves in the sky,
and the seat is made of the jewels
of knowledge:

What subtle threads the woman weaves,
and makes them fine with love
and reverence!

Kabir says: "I am weaving the gar-
land of day and night. When
my Lover comes and touches me
with His feet, I shall offer Him my
tears."

XCIII

III. 111. *koṭīn bhānu candra tārāgaṇ*

BENEATH the great umbrella of
my King millions of suns and
moons and stars are shining!
He is the Mind within my mind: He
is the Eye within mine eye.
Ah, could my mind and eyes be one!
Could my love but reach to my
Lover! Could but the fiery heat
of my heart be cooled!
Kabir says: "When you unite love
with the Lover, then you have
love's perfection."

XCIV

I. 92. *avadhū begam deś hamārā*

O SADHU! my land is a sorrowless land.

I cry aloud to all, to the king and
the beggar, the emperor and the
fakir —

Whosoever seeks for shelter in the
Highest, let all come and settle
in my land!

Let the weary come and lay his burdens
here!

So live here, my brother, that you may
cross with ease to that other shore.

It is a land without earth or sky, without moon or stars;

For only the radiance of Truth shines
in my Lord's Durbar.

Kabir says: "O beloved brother!
naught is essential save Truth."

XCV

I. 109. *sāīn ke saṅgat sāsur āī*

I CAME with my Lord to my Lord's home: but I lived not with Him and I tasted Him not, and my youth passed away like a dream.

On my wedding night my women-friends sang in chorus, and I was anointed with the unguents of pleasure and pain:

But when the ceremony was over, I left my Lord and came away, and my kinsman tried to console me upon the road.

Kabir says, "I shall go to my Lord's house with my love at my side; then shall I sound the trumpet of triumph!"

XCVI

I. 75.   *samajh dekh man mīt piyarwā*

O FRIEND, dear heart of mine, think well! if you love indeed, then why do you sleep?

If you have found Him, then give yourself utterly, and take Him to you.

Why do you loose Him again and again?

If the deep sleep of rest has come to your eyes, why waste your time making the bed and arranging the pillows?

Kabir says: "I tell you the ways of love! Even though the head itself must be given, why should you weep over it?"

XCVII

II. 90.   *sāhab ham men̠, sāhab tum men̠*

THE Lord is in me, the Lord is in
    you, as life is in every seed.   O
    servant ! put false pride away, and
    seek for Him within you.

A million suns are ablaze with light,

The sea of blue spreads in the sky,

The fever of life is stilled, and all stains
    are washed away ; when I sit in
    the midst of that world.

Hark to the unstruck bells and drums !
    Take your delight in love !

Rains pour down without water, and
    the rivers are streams of light.

One Love it is that pervades the whole
    world, few there are who know it
    fully :

They are blind who hope to see it by
    the light of reason, that reason
    which is the cause of separation —

The House of Reason is very far away !

How blessed is Kabir, that amidst this
great joy he sings within his own
vessel.

It is the music of the meeting of soul
with soul;

It is the music of the forgetting of
sorrows;

It is the music that transcends all coming in and all going forth.

XCVIII

II. 98. *ṛitu phāgun niyaṛānī*

THE month of March draws near: ah,
who will unite me to my Lover?

How shall I find words for the beauty
of my Beloved? For He is merged
in all beauty.

His colour is in all the pictures of the
world, and it bewitches the body
and the mind.

Those who know this, know what is
this unutterable play of the Spring.

Kabir says: "Listen to me, brother! there are not many who have found this out."

XCIX

II. 111. *Nārad, pyār so antar nāhī*

OH Narad! I know that my Lover cannot be far:

When my Lover wakes, I wake; when He sleeps, I sleep.

He is destroyed at the root who gives pain to my Beloved.

Where they sing His praise, there I live;

When He moves, I walk before Him: my heart yearns for my Beloved.

The infinite pilgrimage lies at His feet, a million devotees are seated there.

Kabir says: "The Lover Himself reveals the glory of true love."

C

II. 122.   *kōī prem kī peṅg jhulāo re*

HANG up the swing of love to-day!
Hang the body and the mind
between the arms of the Beloved,
in the ecstasy of love's joy:

Bring the tearful streams of the rainy
clouds to your eyes, and cover
your heart with the shadow of
darkness:

Bring your face nearer to His ear, and
speak of the deepest longings of
your heart.

Kabir says: "Listen to me, brother!
bring the vision of the Beloved in
your heart."